The Driver, The Journey, The Fall

THE DRIVER, THE JOURNEY, THE FALL

Lisa M. McDougald

RAVEN SHADOW PRESS
LOS ANGELES

The Driver, The Journey, The Fall
© 2018 by Lisa M. McDougald

All rights reserved. This book or any portion thereof may not be reproduced or used in any manner whatsoever without the express written permission of the publisher except for the use of brief quotations in a book review or scholarly journal.

Cover Image, Design and Layout: Lisa M. McDougald

Printed in the United States of America
First Edition: 2018
ISBN (trade paper) 978-1-949268-00-3
LCN 2018907792

Raven Shadow Press
26893 Bouquet Canyon Rd Suite #C-239
Saugus, CA 91350
www.ravenshadowpress.com

Several poems in this collection are previously published on SoloGenXwarriors.com, owned and maintained by the author.

This is a work of confessional poetry. Occasionally, some poems are slanted toward creative interpretation rather than specific context. Certain individuals and circumstances of events have been changed to respect privacy. These are the true feelings and sentiments of the author.

For Aunt Linda ~
you are my sunflower
in a grey world.

I grant myself the serenity
to fully express my inner voice,
courage to assert my outer voice
and acute wisdom
to know the difference.

CONTENTS

Acknowledgements .... *xiii*

Foreword .... *xv*

I.

Broken Bicycle *18*

Zen Park *19*

I'm Not Dumb *21*

Carbon Footprint *22*

Absolution *23*

Lost My Heart *24*

The Other Girl *25*

The Valley of Memory *26*

Sleeping Parents *27*

Blue DNA *28*

Dig *31*

Papa Goes to Church *32*

The Funeral *33*

Unarmed Souls *34*

Worn-Out Boots *35*

The World Is *36*

II.

Path of Pluto *40*

Truth *41*

Stay Awake *42*

Some Kind of Exquisite Place *43*

I Forgot My Wallet *44*

Lovely Things Making Pretty *48*

April 15, 1912 1:50 A.M. *49*

Tragic Manipulations of Spring 50

Paperless Society 51

After the Recession 52

She Marches 54

Next Month 56

Money Matters 57

Things With Wings 59

El Niño 60

Invention of Age 62

Rebecca 63

Love in Pixels 67

Nowhere Station 68

Phone Call at Midnight 70

Haunted Poet 71

III.

Settled and Frayed 74

I Fly into the Sun 75

Dripping Schisms 76

Burn the Fires 77

Intruder 78

Monarch Grove 79

Cape Blanco 80

Sun Rivers 81

Tilting Axis 82

Shadow behind the Clouds 83

Summer Jazz 84

100 Years from My Death, I Hope 85

Small Hands 86

THE DRIVER, THE JOURNEY, THE FALL

Acknowledgements

I would like to thank my sixth grade teacher, Lisa Schour, for her compassion and belief in me; my graphic design professor, Muneera Spence; my writing professors at Oregon State University; Laurel van der Linde for pushing me to attend her advanced writing classes; my wonderful and talented classmates at UCLA Writers' Program, George M. Behe for historical direction; Tell Tell Poetry | telltellpoetry.com for their meticulous editing and suggestions; and my dearest aunt for encouraging me and without whose help this book would never have been completed.

Thank you all for your patience and guidance and faith in me when I thought I wasn't good enough.

Foreword

I began writing poetry in eighth grade. I had a desperate need to express myself through words on paper that I could not speak out loud. Words became a buffer that kept me safe from the chaos of the world.

I struggled through high school. I lacked focus in class. Rather than taking notes, I explored words of death and depression in my spiral notebook next to sketches of surreal, dystopian landscapes, shadowy skulls and Depeche Mode lyrics. I explored my own mortality, frustrations with my parents and anxieties of the future.

I never matured in the manner of conventional norms and over the years, I learned how to nurture myself, developing a kind of survivalist self-esteem. There is so much to explore in this life and my curiosity made me ambitious enough to make it through college. Since then, I played cat-and-mouse with careers that never suited me.

I wrote the majority of poems in this collection for myself, to feel grounded and make sense of what was going on around me. At the time, I was not writing for an audience. Reading my own words provided a sounding board. I began to trust the words. If I slowed myself down just enough, I could reflect the truth of things, record the pain and validate my experiences. The following poems capture events, reflect the inner self and portray the relationships that shaped my life.

I.

Broken Bicycle

Twisted, leaning
against the rail;
tangled chain,
empty frame.

Still locked up—
crumbling rust

red paint chips
weather whips
into the wind—
cul-de-sac ends.

Zen Park

I think of nothing,
pumping legs
backwards, against
the wind.

The trees in
front of me
get small, disappear
in my hair.

Sun filters
lime green through
shuddering leaves.
I push—
leaning forward.

I swing high,
backdrop of blue
outlines, treetops,
shape of thoughts
returning—whoosh!
Boom box laying in the sand,
Doppler effect,
music careening

I slow down the pace,
swaying against
the chains,
staring down,
the texture of
my shoes;

lulling, blood
rushing, dirt swept,
skidded path, numb
sway, drift, hang,
soft, light breeze.

Cassette tape
clicks—
Music stops.
Silence whines.

Wind whispers
should I ditch
another class?
Mom won't mind;
she has cancer.
Rewind the tape.

I'm Not Dumb

A dragon inside her,
    raised and fuming.
    She felt skin
    blister,
    poke beneath.

The wrong change,
    an honest mistake.
    He scoffed
    as if to say,
    That's the problem with women,
    they're not too bright.

She raged.
    The old patron slugged
    toward the door,
    shaking his head;
    last customer of the night.

The dragon pierced the walls
    of her shell
    with talons
    scraping and tearing.

Carbon Footprint

Eyes grasp the moon,
awake in darkness,
wanting to change
my orbit.

Search for answers
amongst the craggy dust—

abandoned. Waterless.

The earthly one
I love,
teary sphere
gravity pulls.

Poison of my species
consumes all I know.

Up in the star fire
I ache to join
the cosmic particles.

Absolution

I murdered him
with the curve
of my lips,
grinding hips,
dredged my nails in
his slippery back.

Not for procreation,
I wanted absolution—
cast off Mother,
spit out Father;

annihilate
the rotting pavement,
vanquish
the impurities,
burn the
void.

Lost My Heart

It fell on the floor,
seeped into
the shag carpet,
rolled under the maize
colored sofa.

I crawled under
but the Siamese
cat batted it back
toward the floor
furnace, knocking
over Dad's brown
boots, and rolling
out the door.

I tried to stop it;
it rolled down
the driveway and
dented its side
against Mom's
VW Beetle,
landing next
to a Poplar tree.

I picked it up.
It was full of dirt
and pine needles
and ladybugs
and .22 shells.
I placed it back in.

The Other Girl

The grey covers me in thick tar
on rooftops in spring.

It punches through and the seal breaks.
I can't breathe. I lie restless in my coffin.

The boy is held hostage in another universe where
there is no light. I feel him through channels.

Gloom pits the pavement running deep into cracks
that open into the underworld.

Grey eats the color in the display case;
fruits shrivel and turn black.

Somewhere in the darkness he calls to me.
I can feel the cold in his bones.

The Valley of Memory

Smoke billows out from the campfire
in wispy and ethereal blooms.
Shadows flicker at the flame.
I wander through caverns,
stepping over rivers caressing the land.

Your face appears in rippling water;
waves distort you.
A forgotten world reemerges
cleansed in springs of time passed.

From treacherous waters now calm,
buzzards watch overhead, and my soul passes
through the underworld; cracked and gaping,
memory flooding in.

Atop a cliff, you stand gazing down at me,
skin like pale limestone, sobs like
rolling thunder, pouring rain in sorrow.
I disappear into the shiny pools.

Sleeping Parents

I swing on rooftops, smoke cigarettes on
    sunbaked tiles,
        lurking, leaping, thinking

until dawn greets me;
    blinding light,
        it corrupts the air I breathe.

I lack the strength to counter, so up I come,
    out from my bedroom,
        odd creature of the night.

I seek a thread of light looking, on and on,
    through the blackness,
        into the abyss of reason.

Swelling in pools, blackened ooze,
    distant horizon,
        dirty orange turns grey;

sweltering in sunlight, my body melts.
    The vultures come,
        groaning and salivating.

Smell of bodies sinking in sand, losing water;
    dreary existence,
        parents waking up, back to bed.

Blue DNA

Bundle of veins,
blue—
swelling in stains,
the heart
pumps the color;

no oxygen,
self-doubt,
sadness thickening
out.

Black tendrils
grow near my vessel.
Fighting shrills
stop.

Purge the feeling,
shift the body,
stop the reeling,
yet—

the feeling is
threatening in
abysmal coats of
midnight gloom.

Nothing inside,
not fit to be in
this world.

Consciousness
breaks;
summoning
the blood,
eternal—
blue glut.

The wet escapes.
No fortress there
to hold.
Retreat—it goes
under the skin.

But the world will
creep in,
crowding the soul;
the mind, remote.
Now.

Twitching, grasping,
growing wild,
breathing, too
fast.

Deep in sorrow,
cutting the bones.
Ivy punctures
visceral holes.

DNA smells
putrid, soiled.
Become something
else.

Dig

Where is the damp?
Must find it soon.

Staggered limbs.
Soiled blood.
Dark will come.

Animal.
I shelter
under earth.

Cool in dirt.
Wet in cave.
I am safe.
I must dig.

Worms slide
beneath
corpse weed
trenches.

The hands dig.
Dig, dig, dig.

In blackened sky,
there is no more.
Must crawl inside,
the drought is here.

Papa Goes to Church

His hands were tree trunks,
short, stubby fingers, suspender straps;
we called him Papa like the sound
smoke makes coming out of a chimney,
Willie Nelson twinkle in his eyes.

He paid no taxes, faithful man of God;
Bandito follows with the sweep of his tail
out into the woods to dig up turnips.
Earthworms pry from below the forest floor.

A far-off whinny, a wild eye pony
around the hill and cast in shadows.
Splash, his horse, loved turnips,
carrots, all discarded vegetables.

In his shop, the compressed air breaks
the quiet of the bluebird's den.
Some say Papa had gold buried somewhere in that isolation,
where no man in winter may tread the hill.

The Funeral

Three bullets sound in unison.
He loved you if you were Christian.

His grey face sunk toward the ground.
Director says he was special. Unbound.

Lowly and softly the moisture rose
in amber sunset, bitter woes,

with a sudden feeling so deeply hidden
to bury your Grandpa—well ridden.

Over and down the side of that hill,
where great trucks thunder still

with forested cargo around the bend,
a sigh of relief. No more forbidden.

Unarmed Souls

Doomsday clock—
it won't be long.

Set up shop,
have some kids,

remodel the house,
change out the drapes.

Duck and cover
under the desk.

No weapons to fight,
boot in face.

Dig your grave,
get your fix.

Make a will,
last romance;

in walks Huxley,
dead man's party.

Two minutes to midnight,
one last dance.

Worn-Out Boots

As a child sheltered from life,
I stand awake threatened by strife.

Nestled within my troubled heart
I hold my hopes for a new start.

My tears now dry and gone,
I stand firm my soul has won.

I see my future in new light;
dreams flow, flickering candles at night.

Memories that wrenched my troubled mind
have been frozen and left behind.

I walk confident and proud,
eyes never drifting to the ground.

I am alive. My soul is free.
The future is mine for all eyes to see,

old jeans' hanging strands,
on my feet I stand

forever.

The World Is

The light invades the great world,
    a cliff falls from an ancient land,
and all that is real is the sand and nothing;

nothing falls into nothingness
and becomes a flower thrusting out of a soiled prison.

    Dreams plunge into rivers, flow into oceans,
and something leaps into somethingness.

II.

Path of Pluto

I explore waking matter—
precious, dreaming stars.

Cold and desolate, far away,
I am a small planet—like Pluto.

I shelter a big name,
stepping with small footprints.

My orbit is large,
crossing lone comets.

I seek oxygen in space.
I seek unknown domains.

I am a small planet
hunting enlightenment.

Truth

I am the disease that penetrates the cell.
I am the creature that screams its hell.
I am the tempest that floods the darkness.
I am the flame that flirts with the abyss.
I am haunted because I am dead.
When alive, I suffer instead.
I am the one who watches the world.
I am the one who wakes the absurd.

Stay Awake

Snowflakes melting on
a rotting corpse.

Hope stops the mind.
Primal instincts lift
up the small space of
unknowingness.

Survival in
limitless shifts
temper and probe
the dark corners
denying death—

wiggle and thrash
powerful waves;
the brainstems quake.
Hope is what trips
us from sleep.

Some Kind of Exquisite Place

Puncture that place
inside of me.
I feel you,
in the desperate hour,
ejaculate,
sense of power
that only gives
a kind of relief.

Relief is short.
Nothing, really.
A shiny space you think of,
some kind of exquisite place
where ultimate feeling sticks.

You fear nothing
in the moment.
Relief is gone.
Let it be lost.

Nothing is void and vacant.
Nothing is pregnant with air.
Nothing is something you want.
Nothing is plenty and not.

I Forgot My Wallet

I can't help that things
keep happening—
a roller coaster ride
with no safety belts.

How did I get here?
I could use
a pap smear,
a mammogram,
a teeth cleaning—
but no one tells you
how much it will cost
and I must buy wine.

Am I obsolete?
Did I fall
through a crack
in my generation?

I hold on;
inertia spins
me off.

I float
far away.

I land
with a bang
into another
amusement

park. I forgot

my wallet and
have to crawl
under the fence.

A window—
people inside
looking normal.
I think they
are made of bugs
with latex skin.

I feel
the rain and hope
I get
somewhere.

On the deck,
the ants pass each other,
a pheromone highway.

Ground squirrels sniffing
each other's butts
under the tail;
flower opens up,
sharp beaks
of hummingbirds
shop for the best,
pretty pink fluff.

Cheating lovers.
Soft petals.

The soft turns brown
around the edges;
the color fades.

The wind knocks
off the worn and hard
onto the deck next to
a bumblebee corpse.

Oh, what my imagination can do
with flower fluff and bumblebee corpses—
Salvador Dali
painted dreams.

I am a rotting vagina
sitting next to
a dead bumblebee.

Lovely Things Making Pretty

Leave a seed until the world is
full of pretty things
I must penetrate.

There's another pretty thing
I must penetrate.
I need more—

lovely homes
and pretty blood
on battlefields
and lovely, slick engines
and landfills of pretty

Wal-Mart wares and
Cabbage Patch
dolls
and lovely plastic
floating on seas
filled with pretty dolphins
upchucking old tires
and my neighbor's iPhone.

April 15, 1912 1:50 a.m.

I'll put in a complaint tomorrow.
Why is Father not getting in?
Surely he is important—
and brother is younger than us.

This is temporary.
There is no real danger.
Nature can't possibly
halt this adventure.

Ridiculous, this is.
This ship is unsinkable.
Something is
tilting;
must be the
champagne.

Everything is fine,
the engines will go
and we'll be off this
silly, little boat.

It's cold and I want
to go to my room,
take a peek at my
trousseau.

Tragic Manipulations of Spring

When we see the future, our eyes see the refraction of our past.
Rectified and disillusioned with unmistakable fury, we look upon
our being as a resurrection of our innocence.

Shoved into disbelief and tragic manipulations that feed
upon our gardens like plagues of locusts. Our minds are filled with
regurgitations of the ghosts

whose ideals prey upon the souls of our ancestors.

I embrace the lies, pay good money for an institutional education,
the blanket of the unreal that steals away the soul for profit.
I taste the layers of misery like a foul substance—I buck it off.

I am glorified, unchained, a tiger ravaging its kill in the tall,
wavering grass, my existence unfolding like pages in a book. Black
and white fade to a dreary winter in the depths of my eternity.
I am one with my past and future—

    a crystal lake in spring.

Paperless Society

Plastic islands,
poor factories,
assembly lines,
churning product,
cadmium, lead;
souls exploited,

rich men on top
take vacations.
Mind the numbers.
What else matters?

Cheaper to buy,
faster we make,
more toxic waste,
six months or less,
planned obsolesce,

the hole we fill,
the earth falls in,
we all go down.

After the Recession

A young girl,
perhaps fourteen,
slumped in a chair,
her neck stretched down
staring at the screen,
clutching her mouse;

Day-Glo red hair,
black Converse sneakers,
legs spread out,
feet turned in.
I could not help
but conjure
a person from
an insane asylum
pulling against chains;
a twisted mass
tortured, strained.

Her whole body
contorted around
the computer
like rib bones
clinging to liver.

Her face hung
as if some invisible string
was tied taut
to a single nose hair.
So entranced
by her image,

I almost tripped
on a doll
sitting on
the floor
who looked like she might
sever my heel.

Little statuettes of Buddha
grinned amongst
the gothic dolls
with X's for eyeballs.

This used to be
a boutique before—
my aunt's favorite store.

She Marches

Refugees flee from Syrian bombs,
leaving on vessels starved for new homes.

Tears stream down,
need substance now.

Countries packed together,
explosive and prepped to fire.

Leaders are losing their minds,
people consumed by hatred.

Temperatures push up.
Earth is running amok.

2016—what will it mean?

The glue of the past may unravel
and blood will splatter in ritual.

And all that progressed our humanity
will be lost in moments of infamy.

Libraries will die.
Humanity cries.

Progress is dead,
off with our heads.

Same as before,
hunger and more.

Lost again,
to fake and to fend.

No learning from the past,
no future that will last.

I am in my bubble,
secure with no real trouble.

If I exist, then I must try
to do what I can before I die.

I refuse to accept that
all of this world is inept.

Next Month

Check my panties,
red. Soaked through.

Harnessed in madness,
bleeding in pools.

I fight stains
every month.

Some days I hate
everything.

Out of my mind,
control is waning.

I must isolate myself
from people, from men…

clogging, sticky, oozing rage—

I like it when it turns dark,
a sign it's coming to an end,

when I can be good again.

Money Matters

I'm tired of waiting
for good things to happen
as if my thoughts
are what makes it so,

fed up with a world
that nurtures corruption,
where politics destroy
all that is good;

weary of life
controlled by money,
that we cannot change,
that we are locked in.

Watching people
tell children lies—
don't cry, boys, be strong;
smile, girls, get along.

I'm sick of apathy and
spiteful ignorance,
no citizenship,
no restless want of a soul;

money for corporations
that pollute the fields
flood the mind with greed;

my worth compared to
dollars and all the things
I could be don't matter.

I'm sick of you wanting
things that decay and rot joy,
garbage heaps of broken toys.

Money is success;
a strong economy,
good for everybody—

I'm tired of the lies
we tell ourselves
that inherently are wrong
and agree are right.

Things With Wings

You never liked flying things,
things with wings
that fluttered and sputtered.

You were afraid and ran to hide.
So I took the flying things away,
released them out into the sky.

I don't know why
you were scared, so petrified.

One day it rained too long
and my shoulders grew heavy
with weight; I discovered
I could fly
from all the pain,
the emptiness.
I was a thing with wings.

I had to fly away,
away from you.

El Niño

Eyes open wide,
waiting for rain,

promise of destruction,
climate of change.

Why do we yearn for terrible things?
Are we wicked? Are we strange?

And why, because all that is, is not enough.
Comfort is boring and absent of stuff—
stuff that motivates and expands our minds,
manufacturing synthetics to nature's kind.

Eyes open wide,
ready for change—

to get the human race to focus again,
eyes open wide for an end to this end.

The life I want, I declare, I demand

to be as one as one can be
to love the purity of the sea
to love all that crawls and flies
to love all that terrifies and delights.

Beyond my terrible wicked mind—
to love all of nature and its kind,
to govern all with deep respect.
My life is short, but I must confess

that I, in my soul, do feel
that our lives are all too real.
We must fight for all with zeal.

Invention of Age

Time flows through cosmic persistence
only present in human existence,

no destination crosses its steady path,
no rest stops to foil its steady graph.

Never to age like that of mere mortals,
never to change, never grow old.

Time creases the skin and wrinkles the frown,
gravity jumps in and pulls everything down.

Rebecca

I just met you.
The last day of my job,
you just began yours,
panic was in your eyes
at my leaving.

I couldn't tell you
what was happening.
I had to quit,
against a wall.

You gave me a letter.
Your eyes in mine,
a reflection of my
own deep nature.

I kept in touch.
And things got bad,
got really bad.
I tried to help.
You were so much
like me.
But I couldn't do enough.

You must have seen
inside my soul;
I tried to help
on the phone.

We spoke for hours
at midnight while
I smoked cigarettes;
the moonlight passing
over our voices
and you shared with me
the deep well
that was your life.

You wanted things
to change,
to be a better friend,
to make a deeper connection.
I wanted to.
I was afraid.
You were the same.

*I have a small
circle of friends*
you told me.
You wanted me
over for wine,
share stories,
but he was there,
your husband.

He hurt you one night.
In a locked bedroom,
you called.
He was on the couch
passed out.
He punched you
in the stomach.

If only I could have
spent time with you,
traded stories
in real time
like women do,
tears and wine,
holding hands.

Perhaps you would
have seen the fire
in my eyes
that keeps me alive.
Perhaps it would
have lit your pilot
to stay here, to continue.
I wish I could have
helped you.

You tried to be
everything
for your sons,
for your husband,
and you lost
yourself
and took those pills
and left an empty bottle.

I never got the chance
to trade stories
in real time
like women do,
tears and wine,
holding hands.

Love in Pixels

A vast chasm,
I look out at you.
You are delicious
from a distance.

My imagination
makes you into something
and perhaps you do the same
of me.

Yet the world is so complex.
So not right for us to connect.
So unhappy for us to dissent
beyond this Facebook sentiment

to form anything
resembling
love.

The word is pretty,
isn't it?

Nowhere Station

I am tired of keeping something inside.
Too many experiences I never wanted to hold onto,
I never wished to be a part of,
I never conceded to in the beginning,

but I went along for the ride because the car went too fast
before I could know all consequences.

Here I am, many years away and there I was,
standing at the train station.
I was with you and you were with so-and-so and we were
with someone we didn't know and we got on—

no parents around,
no person to care enough,
to tell us we shouldn't do it,
we should not ride this train,
we should not go on this path.

Maybe their words would have stopped us
from doing things that were wrong, the prospect
of doing things that were wrong.

Yet we rode that train,
never thought about it,
never thought there would be consequences
years later.

We rode that stupid train and it took us to nowhere
and left us stranded and heartbroken and still we rode on,
thinking everything was okay. That we could somehow
be whole again if we made it, if we were successful—
trade your soul for a parking spot.

The train let us down.
No one was there to meet us
and we had to get by
and all the things they told us were lies.

Phone Call at Midnight

Don't tell me your secret.
Share it with someone else.

I can no longer be trusted
with your information.

I can no longer plead the Fifth.
I can no longer stop the leaks.

I can no longer share your life.
I can no longer be a friend.

I don't deserve to be in your life.
I don't deserve to hear your secrets.

Pacify the lie;
slip of the tongue
and I've ruined your life.

I have nothing more to give.
I can no longer hold

the poison in.

Haunted Poet

I did not want to seek the truth.
I did not want to feel so used.
I did not want to have to ruse.

Yet it daunted.

I did not wish a feeble start.
I did not wish to be so smart.
I did not wish to prison art.

Yet it flaunted.

I did not want to be a poet.
I did not want to even show it.
I did not want to think I'd know it.

Yet it taunted.

I did not want this tender heart.
I did not want this tragic part.
I did not want this putrid fart.

Yet it haunted.

I did not run so fast away.
I did not run too far and stray.
I did not run from it today.

III.

Settled and Frayed

Wind whips the sullen strands.
Oh my heart beats such grand
notes that
retreat and
hold tight

to earth
in spite
of angry
threats of hate.

I stand bold
and shake.
The fear stalks
against my skin.

It tries to
seep inside my bones
forcing my eyes
open wide.

The fear leaps into the air
my nerves settled
and frayed.

I alone stand, despite fear.
Wind whips the sullen strands.

I Fly into the Sun

I was born
into chaos.
Doomed from the start.
And behold—
I fly

into the storm,
into the world.
I fall

into self-study,
the body, a form.
And out a dragon,

universal truth
flowing in veins
builds into muscle

a raging mass
containing
the dying star.

Dripping Schisms

I dream through enchanted prisms,
lights of darkly dripping schisms,

and as the light pours out of my cells,
I drink in the rays, even if it repels.

My soul shudders to the quick. It burns,
the blood pumping the current in turns.

My breath escapes in a shadowy cough.
Upright and screaming, I finally run off,

over sleeping rocks and threatening trench.
I spurt and sprawl and bleed and wretch

until all cells are raped and dry,
until all tears and anguish subside,

and only the raspy null that exists
do dreams wash over my vessel persist.

Burn the Fires

When all around you falls away,
burn the fires inside your hearth.
Flow the oxygen in your blood,
hold on steady to the earth.

Give only when your soul is free
and only in its truest form.
Keep the flame burning on inside.

As the world threatens to upraise,
let it in to stoke the flame;
shut it out when the winds rage.

Keep that torch on fire,
feed your mind with history,
observe all that is to see,
blaze a path for the living.

Fight for the truth in all things,
hope for the best in all these dreams,
love with the deepest wells of your spring.

Intruder

I saw you in my dream
pulling at the clouds,

picking through tattered shards,
invading my childhood haunts;

sacred playgrounds, runaway places,
the supple glow of smiling faces,

candid whispers from loving lips,
fading light of the moon's eclipse.

Droning voices over silent treetops,
a waning echo above a canyon's drop.

This is my dream.
Let me be.

Monarch Grove

Blue skies,
orange butterflies;
nuances of the day
turn the sky
upside 'round,
zooming in, zooming out.

Microscope,
hanging hope,
a climate
inside my
jeans pocket,
filled with whys.

Cape Blanco

I drink from
the well
of hope.

It fades
and reflects.
Soul water
expanding
into deep
tide pools.

Want
guides the dark
force.

Sun Rivers

And all the years float
like tragic, tepid stars.
Blistering beams and scars
that burn the fuel out of the sun.

Words tickle the mind.
Raging dream currents,
rich textures that bend
and collide.

Rays turn into rivers
and out pours the soul
wandering in desperation,
at large and present.

Tilting Axis

Turn the branch,
shift direction,
follow the sun,
hold onto the earth.

Change the course
through the rain
with blood dripping,
despite the pain.

Love the self
inside the soul—
the driver,
the journey,
and the fall.

Shadow behind the Clouds

Something shifts,
the foundation moves.
A building unsticks.
Conforming rot wicks;

it turns in a new light,
a different color,
shadows falling on the other side.

The gleaming juice—solidified.
I become myself,

a crystal shadow,
and I am new,
sprouting in tangled roots—unhinged.

Raw cracks open before me.
I see without atmosphere,
no weather to shape the cloud.

A puff,
then a doubt,
I fall back into the prison of the world.

Through grating jaws
and quivering fists,
I scream into the endless blue infinite.

Summer Jazz

Amber fades to firelight,
musician plays a solo—
rhythm nudging ecstasy,
shedding clingy, frozen shards.

Pluto jumps into the sun—

love in heating streams flows,
a dream romance unfurls,
lost in longing eyes,
chaotic, blistering vibes.

Notes force the salt,
spilling in yawning wells.
The sand plays with
the desert fish.

Fireflies dance in shadow,
amoebas drain to
the ocean beds.

Crimson pours in,
iceberg melting,
saxophone blares
the grime off summer.

100 Years from My Death, I Hope

it rains in the desert;
water drains to the ocean
compassion overrides commerce

all little girls will be
safe in the world
the beat of native drums
will be heard in storms
punk rock no longer
will be necessary

coyotes will howl,
old books read under trees
sunken tombstones will be
remembered—loved

solar will render
nuclear obsolete,
children will know
tigers, narwhals,
horses, snow leopards;
and the fire
within earth
will burn on.

Small Hands

I shine down
upon the world—
into its void,
into its wake.

      I shine down
      looking for light
      inside the realm,
      outside the noise.

I shine down;
my love grows trees.
My heart swells streams.
Nothingness rains,
sheltered in place.

      I shine down
      upon the world—
      my vengeance makes
      blood sacrifice,
      monthly torment.

I shine down
my desire,
my anger,
my good nature.

I shine down
my love and mind,
my hope and pain;

        I shine down
        my life's work,
        my synergy,
        my essentials.

I shine down
my existence,
my consequence,
my disgraces.

Author photograph by Linda Mae Watson

Born in 1974 in Big Bear Lake, California, Lisa M. McDougald is an author living in the Los Angeles Area. Her work has appeared in *Reminisce Magazine,* the Titanic Historical Society's *The Commutator,* and *NerdWallet,* where she was formerly a contributor. A descendant of survivors on board the *RMS Titanic,* Lisa holds a degree from Oregon State University, manages a blog dedicated to Generation X, and is actively researching her family history and genealogy. She is currently working on a YA novel and several children's picture books. Find out more at *WakingDreamCurrents.com.*

www.ingramcontent.com/pod-product-compliance
Lightning Source LLC
Chambersburg PA
CBHW051709040426
42446CB00008B/797